Question & Answers | A Guide for Startups and Entrepreneurs

StartUp Never Fails

Rakesh Sidana

An Entrepreneur, Mentor, Founder

An Author
"I want to Fly, where are my Wings"
"Where #Share is like Love"

©2020 RakeshSIDANA.ORG | ISBN: 9781660971343

What Others Say…

I have my agency to serve US product based company and I used to read Rakesh Sidana posts on Facebook. His post really impacts me positively on different aspects of the business. Thank

The way Rakesh Sidana shares his experience, I am sure it must be worth reading

Nobody can describe actions and reactions in an Entrepreneur's life so well :-) Each line is amazingly true, Rakesh

What Others Say…

To motivate me and my team. I want to learn every day. I don't stop learning. Just wanna be at the top and still wanna explore more n more. Thank you.

Gone through a small article that you have written and sounded interesting. So I decided to explore further what you have written and it may help to find what am looking for.

Great content! I really appreciate the effort taken to create the course and to publish it. I could personally relate to a few specific points, where I heard the exact words I needed to hear.

TABLE OF CONTENTS

10. I have an idea for a startup but there's already a well-funded startup with the related idea, what should I do?

11. How can I find and meet my first investor for my startup?

12. How can I get investment for my startup when my startup is just an idea?

13. What is the difference between a co-founder and a business partner?

14. How can we decide who will be the CEO when there are 2 co-founders?

15. Is it wise for an entrepreneur to be involved in 2 or more Businesses at the Same Time?

16. Why do people suck at their lives even if they know most of the lifehacks, lessons, and advice?

17. Can the investor reach out to the employees directly for company updates? How does the CEO perceive this?

18. My startup is running out of cash, though I haven't started pitching, an angel investor is interested but taking longer than expected. What should I do?

19. I was a co-founder of a company that I left because of a difficult relationship with my co-founder that I could not bear anymore. I'm looking for a job now, but how can I be honest about it during the interview?

20. How does an entrepreneur know when it is time to exit from a startup?

What do most
startup founders
waste their time
doing?

In India, startup Founders waste time doing the following :

1. Reading every PR of funding thinking they will also become quick rich. (Most of the PR are paid and they don't check how much money has been invested or in the bank.)

2. Chasing Investors who say "I like your idea but I am traveling, will surely fund your idea" (after 1 year, they are still in touch but no fund in the bank).

3. Attending every startup event for advice. Ask the same question (how can I ...) to all senior people and made all of them mentors

4. Spending too much time on Social Media and...

   ...forgetting the Target Customer.

5. Giving Advice that really consumes time as you want others to learn from them.

6. Become a SPEAKER before "unrelated" audiences.

7. Taking interviews. Even this is a must but consumes lots of time and business may get slow when the founder spends too much time on hiring.

8. Resolving disputes between co-founders.

   When I launched my startup in 2008, there was no revenue for first two years and I wasted lots of time doing similar things till an investor from Mumbai asked me 10 questions in the email and I replied in a minute and he found it interesting and my startup was funded within 3 months.

"Smart Investors don't waste time"

Even the founders waste lots of time doing many things, but this is how they LEARN. Entrepreneurship is a journey and 90% of startups get failed and they lack MOTIVATION just because society doesn't accept entrepreneurship as a career so they need to spend TIME here and there for motivation.

I have a Startup
Idea, how do I proceed?

Start. Start and Start....

Majority of people who have Amazing Ideas but they don't START   Those ideas die in the mind before it comes to the "real" world. Go back to the year 1973 (my birth year) and I couldn't imagine these ideas....

"driverless cars"

"bullet trains"

"robots"

"Facebook"

Any idea can shape "real" when it is STARTED and executed otherwise it will remain as an idea.

Why the majority of people don't start?

1. People laugh at you when you tell them your idea. You don't have people around who can say "YES" and motivate you. (Actually, they laugh on you because they tell you THEIR LIMITATION not "yours"

2. There is no resource to build your idea and you have to RESEARCH. The resource can be anything like a #TEAM, Computer or Product and also includes your "skills" as a resource. My team is my asset.

3. You don't have a mentor or a guide. I know it's NOT EASY to find a mentor when you ask for ADVICE from every senior person and visit every #startupEvent and meeting all seniors. In my case, my first entrepreneur-turned-investor was my mentor because he runs 3 companies, two failed, one sold to Silicon Valley. Thanks to him whatever I know today "The Real" just because of him only. Even you can travel your journey alone but #mentor will make that easy and enjoyable. I remember when we both become friends, he started reading "my silence" over the phone when nothing was working   Find Mentor today.

What you should do to start?

1. Research on your ideas.

2. Search on Google.

3. Finding answers from Quora

4. Sharing on Facebook.

5. Networking on Linkedin.

After doing the above tasks, I am sure you would have replied to the following questions

1. About The Real Problem (is it a real or big problem)

2. The Solutions (existing somewhere or you are the first one)

3. The Business Plan (where is the revenue to sustain or how to be #rich)

4. About The Market (where you can scale fast)

5. About The Investor (which investor to reach for your idea)

START TODAY!

Which is better to do? Either do a job or start up a business with the Same Knowledge.

Everything is better if you are doing what you enjoy. When a great Job is satisfying and you are enjoying your life, that's the best thing that happened with you.

Building business needs multi-tasking whereas Job is assigned in one particular area or field to make you perfect doing that one-thing.

The people leave the job and want to do business when they are not finding themselves doing what they want to do or they are not satisfied with the job.

When they mostly are not satisfied with the job, they look for doing business. Doing business means you have to do multiple tasks yourself and learn while doing and have chances of failure of YOU. On the job, you only don't fail but the TEAM if anything goes wrong.

Job is better if:

1. You are happy with what you are doing. (you have a DreamJob with the knowledge you have)
2. You have the best relationship with your seniors and the team. (You have made best friends at work)
3. You are growing and learning on-the-job.
4. Obviously, getting paid on-time. (I believe in 1st date of every month, that really motivate all employees, but 7th would be ok)

Business is better if:

1. You don't know the tactics of pleasing your senior or you couldn't make your senior happy by following them or their expectations.
2. Your work at the job is not enjoyable and you can't manage pressure.
3. You have a great idea and you enjoy working yourself and can build own team.
4. You are good at multitasking and enjoy doing business.
5. You think you can earn more than your last job salary.

When I left my last job in 2004, I couldn't see my growth for a leading position in the last company. I couldn't wait. I knew I have many other qualities. So, I left and started own "web consultancy" as a freelancer. I was doing business with people around the world. I used to sleep with my laptop talking to Japanese, then Australian, then the UK and USA, working round the clock and ENJOYING with International Business. Later when the dollar started fluctuating and PayPal had a problem with Indian Banks for transfers, my business got slow and I launched a new business in 2008 that become popular and awarded as The Best Business Plan by prestigious management institute IIM-A and have offices across India.

All the best!

#ASKrakeshSIDANA

Why do 95% of Startups fail within five years

For any startup, the first three years are very crucial because it goes through "validation" of concepts, minimal viable product (MVP) and there are more experiments before you understand your STRENGTH to build a large Valuable Product or Service.

Here are "some" of the reasons why startup business fails:

1. Lack of the Right Team and Optimal Performance. Even if you think you have the right team, getting the right OUTCOME is the challenge and there are greater chances of wastage of resources in the first few years. You distribute salaries with the excitement of becoming your own boss.

2. Co-Founder Differences and Disputes. It is not easy that all cofounders are like-minded. More than 3 co-founders mean a lack of understanding and taking a decision is not easy. Even sometimes two co-founders don't make the right decision.

3. Follow and Take advice from everybody and Don't find (and respect) mentor Mostly, think their investors are great mentors. Nobody tells them that investor is investor just because their skills are to INVEST and ROI, not to Mentor to run your business. Recent studies say, best VCs don't intervene and let the founder do what they want to do "themselves" (sometimes no advice required).

4. No co-founder has Selling skills. If you are CEO and you don't know how to sell, there are fewer chances of success or you have to LEARN sales. The startup is a business and it does not run with innovation only, (even it's required) but SALES make the cash flows in.

Enjoy! Be Successful.
#ASKrakeshSIDANA

What are the correct things you did for your startup that made your startup successful?

I launched my startup in 2008 as Unique Business in India, awarded by IIMA, didn't work for 2 years as I was first to do and had NO MARKET. The idea started getting acceptance in 2010, got funded later and now over 100 (estimated) startups are trying to do the same in different cities.

I did the following things correctly:

1. **VALIDATION**: Minimum "Valuable", Viable Product (MVP). Nothing works well until you do TEST with the market if that will work or not. You have to check if people will pay for your product or service and how much they will pay. Even you think your idea will change the world but if nobody accepts and pays you, you can not survive. Even Investors do separate TEST and get stats from their dedicated team if how much your startup can grow before they invest in your startup.

2. **FOCUS**: I didn't lose focus on what I want to bring VALUE to my customers. Even I failed many times but the mission was still the same to provide the SAME service with CHOICE for customers and Saving their money.

There will be many people around you to ask you to quit but only you know "what you want to build". Never Stop ☐ Focus. While doing small tasks, building team, operational level stuff, losing focus is very common and especially when you have NO CASH in the bank and you jump into something that creates CASH and forgets what you were trying to build. There can be temporary HOLD but when you have money come back to what you want to do. Smart Investors always understand this stuff of losing focus in operational stuff.

3. **NETWORKING**: Meeting people must be your hobby ☐ You will get everything from this world, people give you ideas, support, funds and REACH ☐ You should be in touch with everybody in your circle even if you are not doing well and struggling. I got all my funding rounds just having casual discussion who connected me to relevant people.

4. **SHARE**: Like I am sharing my ideas here, I share with everyone. I have written two books and speak on many startup events and invited as Guest Lecturer by top institutions of India like IIM, NIT and Management institutions.

Hope this is helpful.
#ASKrakeshSIDANA

What do you want to be? A Businessman or An Entrepreneur.

What's the difference?

Here is a story (in parts)

Part-1:

In 2004, I left my last job, I thought I can do MORE than current job. I became a freelancer. I was hired as a Virtual Employee for a firm in California for 6 months before I started m outsourcing firm for clients globally. Then my work used to bid on online projects, built websites and got paid sitting at home. Learning from other bidders, more I bid on projects, more I used to get projects. To get profit, I just need to try raising a bid for the same project by judging the pocket of the client (budget estimate). If accepted, profit just flowed in. Things were cool.

Am I a businessman or an entrepreneur? Let's find out more.

Part-2:

…then I built a team of programmers, designers. Same work, same bidding site. I was my own boss. Bidding on projects regularly, it became a habit. Working round the clock meeting Time Zone of Japanese, Australian, UK, and the USA, I used to sleep late. Routine continued. I got the "Top Coder" position (Rating 9.75 out of 10.00) and was "top 100" out of 1 lac Indian coders on that bidding platform. The technology was changing every 6 months and getting coders were not easy and had to pay higher salaries to get top coder.

Am I a businessman or an entrepreneur? Let's find more... Read more...

Part-3:

At that time, Payment Gateway had an issue with Indian banks, the business was difficult. I was finding new things to do. In 2008, I started a new venture for India. I didn't know A, B, C of the automotive industry. I found myself I was the FIRST one to work upon that idea.

The idea was to bring all Car Mechanics and workshops on one platform. I was attending Startup Event and Researching on Google about the Trend in the automotive industry, meeting investors. As the idea got some tractions, media started writing on this UNIQUE IDEA and I was on the cover of much leading newspaper, appeared on TV. First two years, there was no revenue (I was still running my bidding firm but that was declining and survival was difficult). I got some tractions in 2010 and also got funded in 2011, then again got funds in 2013.

Am I a businessman or an entrepreneur? Let's find more... Read...

Part-4:

Every year, I launched Unique and Innovative initiatives and pivoted the Business Model (that's the pain of being FIRST) I started a partnership program in 35 cities. Today there are 100 (estimated) startups trying to do the same in major cities and many fans and followers.

Am I a businessman or an entrepreneur? Tell me? Read more...

Here is the difference:

1. Businessman "prefers" to start SAME what others are doing whereas the entrepreneur is always FIRST to start and others follow their ideas. (If they want to create COPY, nobody can bring out the BEST version than an entrepreneur.

2. The businessman is market players, they jump into the existing market whereas the entrepreneur is market leaders. Entrepreneurs create NEW MARKET.

3. Businessman starts from "money" and "profit" is motivation and sell "values". Entrepreneur creates " values" and looks for "money" later.

4. Businessman follows existing solutions and avoids experimenting. Entrepreneurs always try to "add value" to existing solutions and more tendency to innovate.

Am I a businessman or an entrepreneur? Tell me Now! Comment, please.

Enjoy! Best Wishes!
#ASKrakeshSIDANA

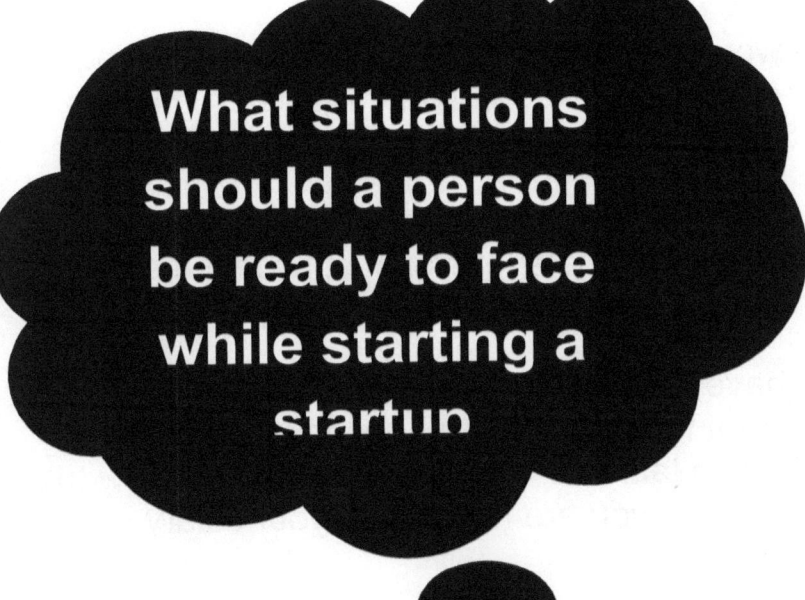

Like life has ups and down, Startup Life is the same.

1. People would laugh on you and you feel bad about it.

2. You have to put your own money, your first RISK if nothing works.

3. You would be spending all of your time working in your startup, your close friend may start missing you. #StartupLove.

4. You don't get the right team initially. It may hurt if your Best Teammate left you just because of less salary and you have to do everything yourself.

5. You have to learn things that you never imagine before starting like... how to hire, how to build a team, how to talk to an investor, how to sell, how to run office even you are not getting your salary in initial days.

6. You think everybody is getting funded but you don't know how to reach investors.

7. You have to face negative customers, that nobody can satisfy. You realize you need to improve on Target Customers.

8. You may get fake reviews and feedback on your services from anybody, jealous of you or maybe your competitors and you are feeling bad about it.

9. You may feel alone when your family doesn't support you and you are not motivated enough but still.... you have to go office daily to motivate your team.

10. Your cofounder don't align with your mindset and vision. You are thinking to shut down every 6 months but you are still running it and searching cofounder.

11. Your growth slows down when you started pitching investors in every Startup Event and you have wasted lots of time, missing office.

Don't be sad reading the above points, here are Great and Good things you will get:

1. You have Happy Customers and they are paying for your expenses. Your Pocket has "own" money not borrowed. Great business relies on repeat customers and loyal they pay you much more than new customers.

2. Your startup has been featured in the local newspaper and family got relieved that you "may" be doing something right. My venture appeared in the media even I didn't know. Recently featured in Gujarat Magazine.

3. You got a solid team that will never leave you even you delay their salaries and instead motivate you that – they are with you when we had no business, I used to know whose team member's LPG gas is empty and I need to give him money to fill it to have dinner at home.

4. You receive calls from Investors and you started learning what is called "valuation", "equity". Your investor meetings are always in 5-star hotels and investors pay for your expenses. Once, my investor pays for my car parking. If you find any of my selfies at 5-star, assume it I am with the investor.

5. You have a Mentor that's giving you good direction and become Family.

6. Your friends are not with you but you have made NEW friends.

7. Your health is sounded well and you sleep well because your team is working hard for you.

Enjoy!
#ASKrakeshSIDANA

What are the best
ways to generate
good business
ideas?

Two major things to look at:

1. The Market & Trend

You must see how big is the market. How many customers you can find to avail of those services like the food industry, hotel industry, and IT industry, etc. Your best ideas would come from "TRENDS". The software industry is changing to SAAS Based and many services would be the " Pay-Per-Usage" concept, even you talk about staying at a hotel, working at coworking space. Whatever idea is working in another country, that has an equal chance to work here.

2. Uniqueness & Need

The unique idea has a chance to survive in a large market if that give at least one value out of these :

- saving

- reduce cost

- comfort

In 2008, when I conceptualized the idea that was awarded by IIMA, it was simply bringing car garages on one platform and I created it to find "why" it is not in India while working in other countries. First two years, there was no revenue, later had few tractions and got funded. It happened just because I knew the TREND of the industry. Then, we had a presence across India. My idea started with "why not" in India. Then I saw the automotive market of 28.6 million registered cars and trends to organize the aftermarket.

To generate the best idea, you must do the following:

Study about the market. If you are a domain expert, you are one step ahead of finding the best idea, but if you are like me (I didn't have industry knowledge) you have to do research and find out about the existing trends.

The problem of the customers. The best idea born out of NEED of the customers. Even your idea is amazing and nobody would buy it, it has no meaning and it will never be the best one.

Solving Large Problems gives birth to a large idea and gives large money. An example is WhatsApp, Google. Customer Behaviour is changing and scaling depends upon the best idea.

I didn't know some people meet me only for taking unique ideas because all my ideas start with "why not"

Enjoy!
#ASKrakeshSIDANA

Is it right for someone to copy my posts and post them without giving credit? One person is doing it regularly.

We must know the reason why we SHARE our thoughts on Fb. Are you educating? Are you spreading Awareness? Are you motivating yourself?

If someone helping you to spread what you write (without mentioning your name) your purpose is still solved. The issue is you want to take CREDIT. I understand your concern. Is it a serious matter? Let's discuss this. Before replying to you precisely, Let me tell you something more.

Today, whatever you are thinking or sharing, at the same time somebody in another world also thinking the same. It does not mean what you know, other don't know, probably some have same knowledge or information but some are hesitant, some don't write on Fb or some just keep ideas in their mind only, but this is for sure, someone already knows the same thing or similar about what you post.

Answer to your question, not giving credit is like not believing the PERSON but liking that THOUGHT only.

Similarly, many people are "reading "this post but they have many other reasons to NOT click on "like". My 2nd book – "Where Share Is Like Love".

Has mentioned 3 types of users on Fb and one doesn't care "like", they are readers, 2nd are Fans who "like" even without reading it some time and 3rd are brainy and think too much, do analysis of before take any action (even that is just a "like"). Like the above example from my book, you can not force people to give you credit for a thought.

Here is a trick to TRY if you want somebody should not copy or give credit :

Start appreciating the same guy who copies your posts.

Every time he copies and paste, just like "love" icon and write any "appreciating" comment. When you do it every time. First, he noticed you are very humble even he is copying, second he would feel like caught every time.

The idea is "appreciation", **human still can be lured or make him soft by "appreciation"** It looks like everybody need desperately appreciation and we try to imitate others. Many times my posts were copied and had more likes than me (I didn't bother but appreciate them. I still appreciate whoever clicks "share". Try this. Hope this is helpful.

Don't feel bad, and insecure when anybody copy your content or posts without credit, you have more content (INSIDE YOU) than somebody can copy.

"They can copy your Idea, but nobody can copy your MIND"

Enjoy!
#ASKrakeshSIDANA

I have an idea for a startup but there's already a well-funded startup with the related idea, what should I do?

You should start the same idea and should be happy because of the following reasons:

1. You have saved money on "experiments" on ideas that are already working.

2. If other startups are well funded, there is still no guarantee if they will survive after spending all the investor's money. Recently on 10th Nov, there is a report released of 121 of the biggest, costliest startup failures of all times (every startup failed after raising $100Million) or you can Google about well funded failed startups.

3. You both are in the same market (boat) and the Market is evolving (aka trend) with a change in customers' behavior who still buys only VALUES. You have to work around those VALUES and build a profitable business.

4. Mostly well funded (mostly) focus on SCALE, that burns the cash and sometime may have enough cash to waste on attracting customers which may not be your TARGET CUSTOMER and bootstrapped (you) always be choosy (selective) to focus on VALUES to become profitable before scaling.

5. This is true that Money helps to sustain or make your profitable after some time but ENOUGH funds lose the focus too. Nobody tells you secretly that well-funded startups also spend money on something that makes their investor happy. I have seen many founders busy preparing themselves all the time for the next round of funding. (raising funds consume lots of time)

6. Last but not the least, you have an equal chance of Raising Fund for yourself. All investors fund only those which already have 2 or 3 competitors to reduce the risk of "experimenting". Interestingly, they follow other investors for investment in similar ideas.

   I felt proud when everybody who copied my startup idea always mentioned it for "Competitive Analysis" for every funding PITCH. Some copied and shut down...and some are doing well. Currently, there are over 100 startups (estimated) are trying the same idea that was first conceptualized by my team.
   In a large market like India, where there are UNORGANIZED markets and big opportunities, everybody has an equal chance to EXPLORE it and PLAY.

   Best Wishes!
   Enjoy!
   #ASKrakeshSIDANA

How can I find and meet my first investor for my startup?

Like you are searching for investors, they are also searching for entrepreneurs. Mostly get only 20% success in finding the right company that gives expected ROI.

Through Media PR.

All funding news has the name of the investors and they also release PR online to let the world know what kind of business they want to fund. Also, they disclose total funds available for investment. You can check their partner's name and search it on Linkedin or their investment firm website.

In 2011, I read news of the launch of a new fund by three entrepreneurs-turned-investors. I got the email from the interview and sent an email and got a reply. This is how I met the first investor for my startup.

Through Startup Events

You can find them in some startup events. There are very popular large Startup Events like YourStory which are organized every year. The motive is to connect entrepreneurs and investors.

I got to know about my 2nd investor while I was waiting for my turn for a 1-to-1 meeting arrangement, which is also called "INVESTOR-DATING", it helps you to sit for a few minutes with the investor. There is a separate session of Funding PITCH before investors.

Even it looks costly sometime, but I think this is worth spending on tickets to meet your First Investor.

Enjoy!
#ASKrakeshSIDANA

How can I get
investment for
my startup
when my
startup is just an
idea?

Getting investment at IDEA STAGE is not easy but possible in the following situations:

1. The idea has already been validated or tested (Minimum Viable Product – MVP) somewhere else but not in your country or city or area.

2. The idea has a big market size and will solve the biggest problem of customers. Big Problem, Big Money.

3. The idea enhances or improves existing proven ideas. The idea can create a New Market.

4. The idea is to align with the GLOBAL TREND and there is large acceptability in the world.

Most investors only fund proven models just to avoid RISKS so that they can get ROI at some time. The idea which can be funded before execution is mostly crowd-funded through some platform to see if that can create some value. In crowd-fund, there are fewer chances of risk of each investor and an individual can take the risk. In crowdfunding, any number (say 10 or 20) of investor can fund the idea to see its Real Value, that divides the risks.

In 2008, even my idea was well recognized and well funded in UK and USA and my idea was awarded by IIMA in 2010, still, nobody funded till it was proven in 2011 with seed Fund then funded in 2013 and I launched partnership program to spread the idea across India for those who are interested to do business in automotive. You can collaborate with like-minded and build initial traction.

INDIA IS CHANGING :

Things are changed now in India. There are Government's STARTUP initiatives and schemes. The people like Shradha Sharma and many who brought ideas and stories of entrepreneurs before investors. The investment at the idea stage is POSSIBLE now.

Build an Innovative Idea!

Don't dream about it...just PROVE the idea.

Best Wishes!

Enjoy!
#ASKrakeshSIDANA

What is the difference between a co-founder and a business partner?

Both could be the same but Co-founder is a specific term and Business Partner is a broader term.

Business Partner could be anybody who is your partner in your business. He would have terms to do business with you. A business partner is more of a professional word for a person who has a partnership on some agreed terms and conditions. He or she could have an interest in your business for a LIMITED time with some limitations on investment or profits.

Co-Founder is used mainly for "startups" and new kinds of fast-growing businesses these days. Co-founders are considered to be Original Group of people who "founded" the startup together and they look like family to each other. They don't limit themselves with terms usually, more like "emotional" tie-up in India and in other countries who put their terms to work together "mutually" to see the growth of the business. They are expected to work together in case of the LOW point of the startup too.

A co-founder is someone who has equity or active interest in the business idea and formation. Sometimes, it can be one of them or both.

Interestingly, when you go for funding nowadays, Investors prefer co-founder's team before investing in your business.

Hope this answer is helpful.
Enjoy!
#ASKrakeshSIDANA

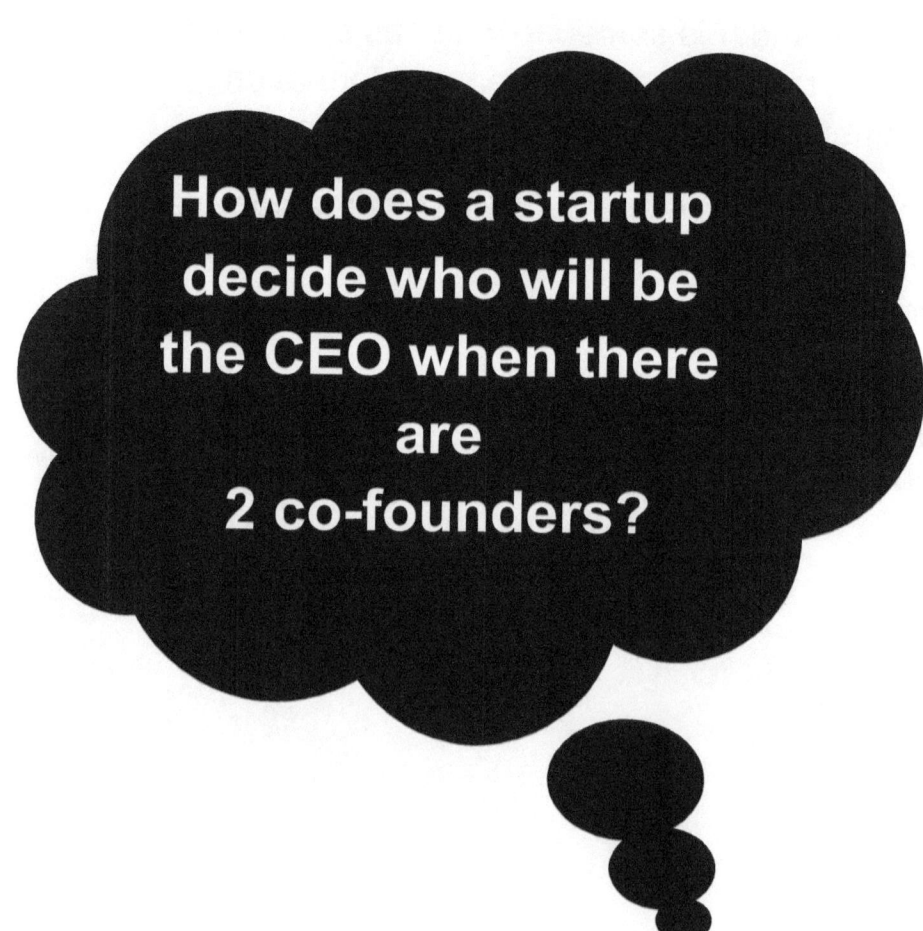

If I change the same question in other words then I would ask one question "who is the leader". CEO is always the leader. Co-Founders mean they are family together and have shared in the business to build a business together. Out of two cofounders whoever possesses high quality for leadership, should be the CEO.

Apart from the domain knowledge or enough experience about the startup idea, you can make a list of the leadership qualities.

He/She knows how to represent the company to the outside world.

He/She should be the best guy for Networking. In modern business, networking is the ONLY key to success.

He/She can manage people better than others because getting great performance from people is not an easier thing. You have to create trust with the team as Co-Founder and CEO. The team members must consider him as a leader.

I have seen some cases where a team is just following CEO just because he/she is the boss but they do not have "acceptance" for his/her leadership. CEO has to be an accepted leader in the organization. You can take feedback from your existing team by asking the question "whom they see as a leader".

He/She should have enough knowledge about Global Trends and what's happening in the other world. He is a more informative guy than others.

He/She also has a great quality of negotiation with team members, vendors, partners, investors, and every stakeholder. Kind of outspoken humble guy.

He/She should know how to raise funds for the startup or he can spend time meeting investors and telling them their vision and current traction and requirements. Mostly, they are good at Financial Stuff also, knowing profit and loss statements.

He/She should acquire Knowledge of legalities so that business can build trust with everybody including customers, investors, partners.

All in all, if you want to know who can become CEO, start writing qualities "those can be acquired – Vs – quality from past events" between both cofounders and give 1 point for each quality from past events. That exercise will give you an answer.

Hope this is helpful.

Best Wishes!

Enjoy!
#ASKrakeshSIDANA

Is it wise for an entrepreneur to be involved in 2 or more Businesses at the Same Time?

It is only wise when "one" business is "set and sustainable" without your presence. My first business started in 2004 was web-development for International clients and started a second business in 2008 parallel that was "India's First Digital Platform for Car Garages". I was investing money from my first business to second new business because first was "sustainable" and I had fix clients that kept me paying monthly and I had delegated most of the work to a senior team even I was getting reports regularly. The second business was a tough, very new and disruptive startup. At one point in time running both was not easy because I was consuming more time with a second business. In 2011, my second business popular with some media coverage, newspaper, and attracted investor's interest.

The investor who wanted to put money into my second business had a condition that I should be focused on new business only and needed a proof that I am not running both.

That was the time I decided to let go of my first business and I sold to my known friend and he was doing good in web development, so I gave them all client access and focus on second business.

Having two business running is wise only when one is doing and sustaining and having profitable Business.

Honestly, if Investor didn't push me for a condition, I could never sell it because I had very good clients from Australia, the USA and some parts of Europe.

Hope this answer is helpful.
#ASKrakeshSIDANA

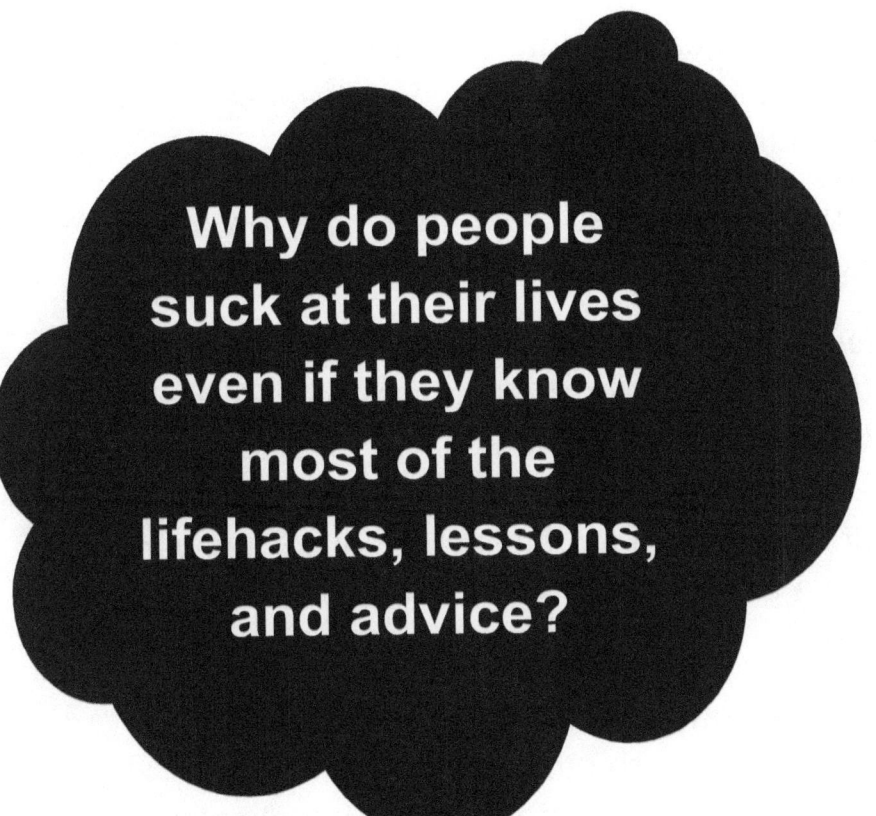

Why do people suck at their lives even if they know most of the lifehacks, lessons, and advice?

They don't do the right things at the right time or they don't have the right people...

TIME has great importance in everybody's life that keeps changing. Advice has no relevance if you minus the moment of doing.

Apart from the "right" time, here are a few more things that impact the lives.

The behavior: Your personality is made up of how you react to situations that matter a lot. All life outcomes are expressions of your REACTIONS at the moment. For example, You reacted wrongly to your boss in the morning just because you were not in a good mood and you were fired from the office.

The knowledge of judging people: We all humans read each other and many-body languages matter. Understanding people play an important part in your decisions and doing business or partnerships with them. For example, you sit with people that hide-intentions and you can get a loss of business from people.

The Right PEOPLE at Right TIME makes a great Successful equation. So, even everybody has access to all kind of knowledge, they still need to learn art of dealing a different kind of people, the art of doing business and the art of "self-motivation" that art of learning does not come just by simply getting advice, you have to learn by doing, exploring and experimenting.

Hope this is helpful.
#ASKrakeshSIDANA

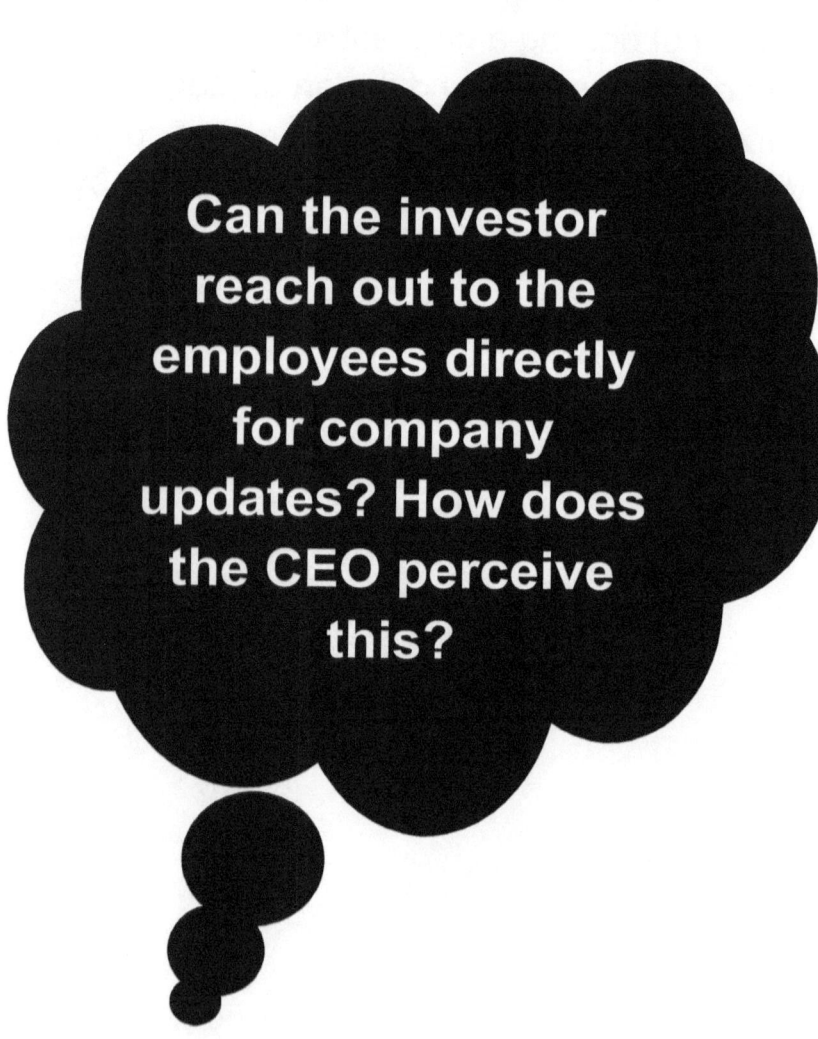

When I got investments for my business, the first investor was entrepreneur-turned-investor and he asked for a call update along with email monthly. Since he was an entrepreneur himself so I discussed with him every weekend to see if I was doing the right things or if any changes required in the business execution. He became my mentor. My second investor was a corporate guy and a monthly email was enough for him with a short call after sending the email.

In both cases, no investor even tried to visit my office. When I shifted my office to a better working place, I invited Investor to have a selfie with my team and he did it once and twice in 2 years.

Investors never intervene in the daily operations if they TRUST you and they know you are going in the right direction. Their main motive is to get ROI from their investments.

Majority of Equity Investments, investors are sleeping (aka non-executive) investors and they only ask for monthly updates.

It is interesting to know why your Investor is too much involved in your startup that he needs to check with employees.

Here are some reasons if your investor is trying to get an update from your employees:

1. They don't trust you and you don't follow them what they are telling you to do again and again.
2. You have given them "Control" right and they are Director with majority share (51%+) on your board and they want to execute your business themselves.

3. They really want to help you by assessing a team's ability or they want to replace you with other co-founder or CEO.

4. They are entrepreneurs and equally passionate like you ☐

My suggestion is that you must build trust and try to understand after meeting them separately (with the cool mind) why they are doing it. Also, check your agreements and discuss them that you don't like them doing it.

Hope this is helpful.

#ASKrakeshSIDANA

My startup is running out of cash, though I haven't started pitching, an angel investor is interested but taking longer than expected. What should I do?

Every business has Ups and Downs but you must set your startup at a stable and sustain level, minimum level. If you are out of cash, which is very common in the early days of starting up, it means you have not figured out what "input" can bring what "output".

Pitching to any Investor consumes lots of your time, so you must know when to start meeting investors.

Investors have own way of looking at startups and they invest in the team, not just ideas. When they take more times and don't say "yes" to you, here are possible reasons :

1. They are talking to many similar Startups silently and you are ONE of them.

2. They are not sure about you as a person, so want to see how you behave or act in the next few meetings.

3. They are talking to their peer Investors to see if they can raise the amount that you actually needed.

4. They don't want to invest as a single or personal capacity, but they want to invest in a group of investors and waiting for answers from other investors.

5. Last reason - they don't have the money yet, but you just chasing them in vain :)

You should not waste your time meeting investors but focus on EXECUTION to see how you can come out of cash crises.

Here are something to come out of cash-crises

Find ways to sell more.

Go to the market and meet more customers.

Don't rely on Sales Guys.

If your product has a great VALUE. Selling VALUE does not need any selling skills. You just need to explain in your own language to Real Customers about your product/service who actually needs it.

Change in the product/service and work upon PRICING. You might be selling Great Value to a poor customer.

Change Target of Customers. Start selling the same with High Ticket Size.

Try ONLINE channels, a platform for BULK Selling. Find your Uncle (Relative or Buddy) in any corporate and switch to B2B model to have cash in your account (even if It's not profitable but you can make it as GMV that you have cash-flow)

Cash is the only King ☐ Not Investor.

Hope this is helpful.

I was a co-founder of a company that I left because of a difficult relationship with my co-founder that I could not bear anymore. I'm looking for a job now, but how can I be honest about it during the interview?

The majority of the startups get fail just because of disputes between cofounders and that's ok. All those who lost interest in pursuing a startup, they join a job in their interest company.

I have seen entrepreneurs are hesitant to join a job just because they feel like a failure. You must accept that Failure is just nothing "unexpected events" that could happen to anybody for any reason. Failure reason can be anything that you got bad team, you put all your saved money into experiments or somebody took advantage of you, etc. I mentioned in my book (I Want to Fly. Where Are My Wings) you need the right people at the right time to generate the right money to become successful.

You should not be hesitant to explain your situation because the company is going to hire you to need people who are honest and LEARN from their failure. Nowadays, many companies prefer startup guys who are failed once so that they can guide them on what not to do to save their cost. Nobody wants to fail, not even the company you are going to join, so they need people who tell them about those problems that you faced. Recently, if you read news of "acquisition" mostly are "acqui-hiring".

There are new trends in the hiring management team by acquiring another distressed startup that is going to fail and have no cash. These Aqua-Hire deals are made to bring failure founders from other startups into successful companies.

To answer you precisely, here is what you can prepare for an interview

1. Tell them your skills, that you couldn't exploit in your startup.
2. What you like the most about your startup.
3. What did you expect from a startup that didn't happen?
4. Now what're your current financial issues (that could be you have to pay EMI of some loan or support your family etc.)

Hope this is helpful.
#ASKrakeshSIDANA

How does an entrepreneur know when it's time to exit?

"Quit" and "Exit" are two terms with a different meaning. Quit is done in unfavorable situations. "Exit" is decided when you have a greater plan of your life after exiting.

I always motivate entrepreneurs to never give up and keep pivoting business model and never exit. I have been executing my Idea for 10 years even when there was no competition in the Industry and I decided to exit. Nobody knows when you need to exit from your startup, it is your call-of-the-moment. It is time when you look beyond the exit. For example, an Investor comes to you to buy your business and you think that is enough money or you think that's the purpose of running your business or anything that can make you rich after exit.

In my experience, some entrepreneurs were not sure of exit, but they took a call at the right time and got a great career after that and I also saw who didn't stop but they bleed their financial situations and broke and then join another company.

Here are some unfavorable situations to tell you that you should stop:

1. There are not enough customers coming to you. The number of customers depends upon the market size. Start from one city and you must know how many customers need your service/product. Not all will use your startup but still, 10% to 20% of the Total Market should be Good Numbers to expect.

2. There is No Repeat Customer. There are always New Customers in the beginning but your startup will sustain on REPEAT customers. You must know when New Customer comes today, need you again. The more the frequency of new customers (if he likes your service/product) using your offerings, there are greater chances of success. If you have an app, you can call "repeat" means "engagement".

3. Nobody is paying you. You can Try the Freemium model where somebody else (advertisers) pay you while others use it for free. For example, nobody pay to Facebook, Gmail for using them but they earn from other channels like advertisements, etc.

4. Your Tech Cofounder betrays you. Sorry to include this, but that is common in India. I found this problem while mentoring entrepreneurs. When you start, make an agreement with your tech-founder that you both keep backup of technologies or apps, etc, in any dispute you could save your Tech-Company.

Leaving aside dispute, the other three are real reasons that tell you must shut down and move-on to another startup. It is Ok. It is life. Have another cup of tea ;)

Hope this is helpful.
#ASKrakeshSIDANA

RAKESH SIDANA
An Entrepreneur, Mentor, and Author

Rakesh Sidana started his Entrepreneurial Journey in 2004 with International Business which served clients all over the world and later he was known for his passion and persistence for his unique Indian business that brought "CHANGE" in the automotive industry. It was first of its kind business to bring SMALL CAR GARAGES and MECHANICS on one platform. This venture brought him in the front for his popularity in the media and he was on TV shows to discuss the change that is going to happen in India in the automotive sector.

He builds new ventures that can impact at large and bring change in the ecosystem.

AWARDS AND BUSINESS MODEL

His unique business model (as per The Economic Times) was awarded by IIM-Ahmedabad and funded by a prestigious investor from Google. Every new startup and automotive corporate now follows his venture before building it for scale. Currently, over 100 startups are following his vision for UNORGANIZED Automotive Aftermarket.

INVESTOR AND MENTOR

He has been on the advisory board of startups and is a mentor for entrepreneurs.

He has been invited and awarded by prestigious institutions like IIM, NIT as Guest Speaker to inspire students with his achievements. He was invited and a part of PM's initiative "Startup India, Standup India".

EVENTS ACROSS INDIA

He organized free campaign all over India by the name of " Startup Never Fails". It was a 1-hour session that he conducted in major cities like Bangalore, Mumbai, and Guwahati and spread awareness about reasons and common mistakes of failures startups.

BOOKS & ONLINE COURSES

He is an author of the book _"I want to Fly, where are my Wings"_ for startups and writes books on recent trends based on his experiences. His second _book "Where #Share is like Love"_ is on Social Media. He is passionate about writing on startup ideas and behavior science. The first book is a motivational book for entrepreneurs with real facts about their life.

To share his knowledge and experiences, he has **online courses** (Udemy) on new technologies and business ideas.

He actively participates in building and engaging startup communities of over 1 lac members.

CAMPAIGNS & SOCIAL WORK

He is also building a Non-Profit group by the name of "I Want to Fly Foundation" for the education of unprivileged kids and offers startups with professionally designed mentorship programs and

BELONGINGNESS & PAST

Migrated from a small town to Delhi for Management course, he started his career in 1997 as an internet executive. Internet was a new term for India at that time and his articles on the Internet and web technologies were published in leading magazines and newspapers like The Times of India.

His passion and persistence for New Technologies lead him to work for large companies. IndiaMART.com was of his first career job which is the largest B2B venture in India.

Follow The Author at the following Links :

Website: http://www.rakeshsidana.org
Facebook: https://www.facebook.com/rakesh.sidana
Linkedin: http://linkedin.com/in/rakeshsidana

Communities :

Join Startup Facebook Communities :
StartupTalky:
https://www.facebook.com/groups/startuptalkygroup/

Startup Never Fails :
https://www.facebook.com/groups/396336554111620/